The Xenophobe's® Guide to The Swedes

Peter Berlin

Ⓞ
Oval Books

Published by Oval Books
335 Kennington Road
London SE11 4QE
United Kingdom

Telephone: +44 (0)20 7582 7123
Fax: +44 (0)20 7582 1022
E-mail: info@ovalbooks.com
Web site: www.xenophobes.com

First published by Ravette Publishing 1994
Reprinted/updated 1996,1997,1998

First published by Oval Books 1999
Updated 2000, reprinted 2001
Updated 2002

Editor – Catriona Tulloch Scott
Series Editor – Anne Tauté

Cover designer – Jim Wire, Quantum
Printer – Cox & Wyman Ltd
Producer – Oval Projects Ltd

Xenophobe's® is a Registered Trademark.

With thanks to *The Swedish Press*, Vancouver.

Though he is shown as the sole author of the
present magnum opus, Peter Berlin wishes
to share the blame with Henrik, Joakim,
Christie and Shirley who helped provide
Swedish insight and Canadian perspective.

ISBN: 1-902825-44-6

Contents

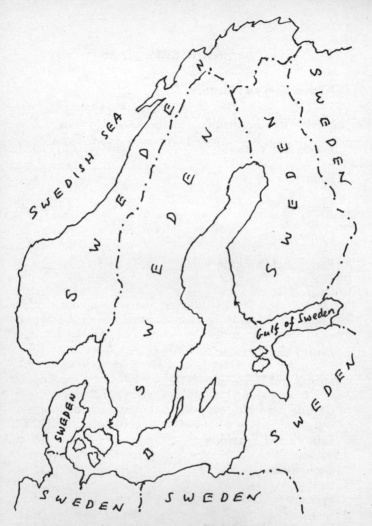

'We thrive on memories of our glorious past.'

The Swedish population is just under 9 million (compared with 4½ million Norwegians, 5 million Finns, 5 million Danes, 50 million English, 82 million Germans and 281 million Americans).

Nationalism and Identity

Forewarned

The Swedes think it entirely appropriate that the cartographer Mercator magnanimously drew Sweden roughly the size of India. They object to being lumped in with other Scandinavians, as if they had no identity of their own.

From a Swedish perspective the differences between the Scandinavian countries are stark. Denmark is horizontal, Norway is vertical, Iceland is melting, Finland is labyrinthian, and Sweden is stunningly pastoral.

There is also the language difference. Every Finnish sentence starts in falsetto and ends in baritone. Norwegian sounds like Finnish intoned backwards but is actually a provincial Swedish dialect. The Danes with their diphthongs, glottal stops and dental fricatives sound as if they are caught between swallowing and spitting out a very hot potato. Only the Swedish language has evolved from grunted Icelandic gobbledygook to become the familiar and beloved orgy-borgy of *The Muppet Show*.

The contrasts in national culture and character are equally glaring. The Norwegians are simple, plain-spoken folk, the Danes cheerful and fun-loving. The Finns are a taciturn lot whose mosquito bites occasionally make them holler and gyrate in what the guide books mistakenly call folk dancing. The Swedes seriously consider that by being hilarious like the Danes, outspoken like the Norwegians and brooding like the Finns, they combine the best of Scandinavian qualities.

Swedes are always surprised to discover that foreigners do not keep a framed map of Sweden above their beds. They are amazed to encounter people who think the capital of Sweden is Oslo, or that Sweden is the home of Swiss watches. Such manifestations of ignorance can only be combated with a concerted campaign of enlightenment which is why the Swedes never tire of lecturing others about Sweden.

There is hardly anything in any other country with which the Swedes do not compare themselves and their country favourably, be it the length of an argument, the breadth of a concept or the height of an audacity. To add credibility, comparisons are usually given a thin patina of self-deprecation but this fails to conceal their underlying national pride.

How Others See Them

The Norwegians believe the Swedes suffer from megalomania, while the Danes consider them to be party poopers. The British perceive them as sexy but cold, and the Germans see them as being rather wet. To the Russians, the Swedes seem just plain thick. Immigrants think highly of Swedish society but deplore the spiritual vacuousness of the natives.

Of course, these perceptions only skim the surface. For instance, the worldwide reputation the Swedes have for being a bit square is misleading, they are positively quadratic. Author Herman Lindquist summed it up thus: the Swedes look at the world through a square frame nailed together by Martin Luther, Gustav Vasa, the Temperance Movement, and 100 years of Socialism. Luther contributed the Swedish taste for simplicity, Vasa the national identity, the Temperance Movement the sanctimoniousness, and Socialism the work-shyness.

The Swedes are reputed to be aloof. As the saying goes: 'You can always tell a Swede, but you can't tell him much'. Ask him a reasonably intelligent question, and all you get in reply is "Huh?" What outsiders do not realise is that 'Huh?' exploits the strategic advantage of asking counter-questions. By forcing the interrogator to rephrase his query, the Swedish respondent is buying time to ponder its dimensions. Did it contain a hidden meaning?

Or, heaven forbid, humour? Behind the façade of eyelash-batting incomprehension the Swedes are merely heeding the maxim 'Think before you speak' or, as the Swedes would put it, 'Blink before you bleat'.

How They See Themselves

The Swedish national anthem says it all: 'We thrive on the memories of our glorious past', a reference to the *Storhetstid*, or 'era of greatness', when Sweden ruled most of Northern Europe (see map). Even earlier, the Vikings had given the peoples around the Mediterranean, on the British Isles and in North America a taste of Swedish brawn. Today's schoolchildren are exhorted to *sträcka på sig* – keep their heads high – when the subject of the Vikings is raised in history class.

Since those heady days, however, the Swedes have made a spectacular about-turn from Rambo to Rimbaud, crusading for a world of innocence while doing a little gun-running on the side. In the 20th century, as nations were tearing themselves apart, the Swedes brokered peace to mend the broken pieces. Raoul Wallenberg, Folke Bernadotte, Dag Hammarskjöld and Olof Palme have gone down in history as dauntless mediators who paid for their audacity with their lives. Inspired by their famous compatriots, the Swedes now see themselves universally as The World's Conscience.

How They See Others

The Swedes are unique in that they do not actually dislike any nationality in particular. The patronising posture they adopt vis-à-vis their Scandinavian neighbours stems not from dislike but simply from the confident belief that Sweden is superior.

Of course they don't appreciate Germans elbowing their way to the *smörgåsbord* on Baltic ferries; or Frenchmen jumping the queue for the ski-lift. But these are considered minor aberrations from the Swedish behavioural norm which is based on conformity.

When travelling, the Swedes prefer to keep the natives at a safe distance by peering at them through the lens of their video cameras. But basically foreigners are good news: their funny faces and foibles help remind the Swedes how wonderful it is to be Swedish and normal.

Character

Melancholy

A common trait among Swedish people is a deeply felt *svårmod*, a dark melancholy born out of long winters, high taxes and a sense of being stuck far out on a geo-political and socio-economic limb. They brood a lot over the meaning of life in a self-absorbed sort of way without ever arriving at satisfactory answers. The stark images and unresolved plots in many of Ingmar Bergman's films are accurate snapshots of the Swedish psyche.

All this *svårmod* makes the Swedes very self-conscious and socially awkward. When two Swedish individuals meet for the first time, there are actually four people present: the two visible persons, plus their invisible alter egos who stand close by and criticise every word and every gesture. Only when the acquaintance is well established do the alter egos move to the sidelines, albeit still shaking their heads.

No wonder then that the Swedes seem aloof, even a little cold, at the first encounter: they are so busy arguing with their alter egos that they cannot focus properly on the company standing before them. But once they emerge from their internal battles, they are capable of friendliness and hospitality to a degree almost bordering on warmth.

Undfallenhet

Another common trait is *undfallenhet,* a tendency to yield under pressure. While their Viking ancestors used confrontation to settle even the most trivial of scores, modern-day Swedes avoid conflict whenever possible. They believe that *undfallenhet* makes for smart strategy. After all, it has kept the country out of war for nearly two centuries and helped it attain one of the highest living standards in the world.

For example, during the Napoleonic Wars, as Russia was about to invade the then Swedish province of Finland, the Finnish conscripts were deeply affected when their Swedish commanders decided to delegate their authority and go home. In World War II, the Swedish government succumbed to Hitler's demands that German troops be allowed to transit through neutral Sweden to sustain the occupation of Norway. To this day, the memory chokes the Norwegians with emotion. The Estonians and Latvians are still incredulous that Sweden once yielded to Soviet demands for the repatriation of Baltic refugees.

In most countries, if a consumer complains about a defect in a product or service he has just bought the salesperson will try to fob him off with excuses. Not so in the Land of *Undfallenhet*. Here the vendor disarms the customer by adding ammunition to his complaint. For example, a customer telephones the firm from which he has hired a car to argue that the studs are missing from the winter tyres and that, as a consequence, he is unfairly exposed to the risk of having to pay for any collision damage. To this the rental agent is likely to reply: "Never mind having to pay for collision damage. What about your personal health and safety?" – and the missing studs are promptly forgiven.

Undfallenhet is not to be confused with cowardice. Sweden has long stood firm on its convictions regarding such matters as apartheid and dictatorship, and has not hesitated to lay down the law to far-away countries like South Africa and Chile. But craning one's neck and straining one's eyes to stare down dictatorship and racism at the other end of the globe is hard work. The Swedes must therefore be forgiven for having overlooked the very same sins being committed for 75 years in neighbouring Russia.

Beliefs and Values

Moderation

When the Vikings took time off, they used to gather around the campfire to down a horn of mead. Though their thirst was great after all their exertions, it became a matter of honour for each warrior to ration his intake so that the horn didn't run dry before everyone had had a swig. In other words, one had to drink team-wise, or *laget om*, later shortened to *lagom*. In modern Swedish the word *lagom* has taken on the meaning of 'just enough' or 'with moderation'.

Lagom permeates Swedish life. It makes round pegs fit into square holes. Economically, it has enabled the nation to find the middle ground between Capitalism and Socialism, i.e. between Progress and Humanity. In manufacturing, *lagom* discards gold-plated designs in favour of optimum solutions. Socially *lagom* puts conformity before excellence, tempers extreme personal wealth and poverty, and leaves the Swedes irksomely at peace with themselves. In short, *lagom* underpins the Swedish Model – not the curvaceous *Playboy* centrefold variety but a contourless nirvana of uniform bliss.

However, the word *lagom* expresses more than just a measure of moderation: it also serves to glorify through understatement. When something is said to be '*lagom* good', it actually means it's the best.

The Swedes firmly believe their country is *lagom* in a variety of skills ranging from invention and training to quality, performance and safety. This strong sense of national invincibility goes back to medieval times when generations of imported bishops were commissioned to invent the history of Sweden. Citing Plato and ancient Icelandic sagas, they proved that Sweden was nothing less than the 'Island of the Gods', i.e. the sunken Atlantis risen again from the ocean floor after the Ice Age with its rich culture surprisingly intact. Not Hebrew but Swedish was the Mother of All Languages, and the runes (ancient carved letters) constituted the very first alphabet.

Moving from fiction to fact, it is true that the Swedish warriors brought down the Roman Empire, ruled the whole of Northern Europe in the 17th century, and in the same period braved the Atlantic to conquer Delaware.

The backwardness of the indigenous Swedish population, which consisted mainly of battlefield gunfodder and illiterate farmers, was overcome by importing Walloon Belgians, Hansa Germans and Bernadotte Frenchmen, in whose hands industry, commerce and administration thrived. Underneath their glacial façade, Swedes display a surprising taste for fire and smoke, having invented dynamite, the safety match and the steam turbine. They also developed the zip fastener to speed up seduction. Anders Celsius, another clever Swede, provided a universal scale for measuring temperature, be it steam or body heat.

Between 1840 and 1920 things became so wonderful in

Sweden that most able-bodied people could stand it no longer and emigrated to America. Those left behind proceeded, by hook and by crook, to build today's cradle-to-grave welfare paradise. No challenge is too great for the *lagom* perfect people.

Pragmatism

In times of trouble, the Swedes always land on their feet. When the world goes to war, Sweden stays clear of the antagonists through a blend of diplomacy and concessions. When the bottom falls out of the economy, the Central Bank raises the interest rate to 500%, devalues the *krona* by 30%, and re-enters the world market with a smile on its face.

When the flagships of Swedish industry feel the pinch of international competition, they merge with their competitors and move their headquarters abroad. In the battle between idealism, heroism and common sense, the latter always wins.

Patriotism

The Swedes sneer at public manifestations of patriotism conveniently forgetting that the blue and yellow Swedish flag is everywhere to be seen – at the top of garden flag-poles, on postcards, on birthday cakes, on the branches of Christmas trees. The colours of the flag are echoed on candles and napkins, on bottle labels and biscuit tins, even on Swedish company logos.

Swedes are not patriots in the usual sense. Victory monuments come in the form of rune stones rather than bronze statues. Ask them what links them to their native country, and they will hold forth, not about government, history or culture, but about deep forests, smiling archipelagos, crayfish served with aquavit, and flower-wrapped maypoles. For Swedes the national flag is primarily an eye-pleasing backdrop. Rather than rallying people to war, it invites them to a picnic in the meadow.

Class

The Swedes espouse the classless society but still get a lot of exercise climbing the social ladder.

Titles have always been important in Sweden. Any title is acceptable, be it Mr., Mrs., Managing Director or Factory Worker. The telephone directory is the prime medium for the Swedes to flaunt class. In addition to their names, titles and principal coordinates, subscribers in the fast lane pay a small fortune to have their little place in the country listed on a separate line. The ultimate status symbol is to reserve yet another line for the mobile telephone.

Another hallmark of class is the surname. There was a time when nearly everybody was called Svensson but, suffering an understandable identity crisis, many re-labelled themselves with etymological misfits such as Sjökvist (Sea Twig) and Granström (Pine Stream). The less imaginative Svenssons settled for laboured spelling variations like Svenzon or Svenzén.

Others took noble- or foreign-sounding name-endings, typically, '-us' or '-born', e.g. Svensuvius and Svenborn. The famous natural scientist Carl Linnaeus was actually born Carl Nilsson and adopted the Latin-sounding Linnaeus in his mid-life to flag his academic credentials. He died even more nobly as Carl von Linné. A country vicar went so far as to endow his parishioners with surnames of the Swedish aristocracy, an act which the genuinely titled tried to overturn in the courts.

The few remaining Svenssons spoiled the class war by inventing the unified class of Medelsvensson, or 'Average

Svensson', the epitome of mediocrity, with the motto *En ann´ ä väl lika go´ som en ann´* (approximately 'Who d'ya think you are?'). For a decade the fun went out of climbing the social ladder. Then, one day, a woman decided to jazz up her husband's undistinguished surname by adopting the Spanish practice of adding her maiden name, thereby introducing the double-barrelled surname to Sweden. The practice quickly became fashionable, and today the Sjökvists and Granströms are being outclassed by a wave of Sjökvist-Wikanders and Granström-Brodins.

The Swedish equivalent of the Arabic Zayed bin Hamad ibn Abd al-Maktoum might be Sven-Valdemar Erik Nils Snoddas Sture Oskarsson-Nygren. Or S.V.E.N.S.S.O.N. for short.

The various classes also manifest different habits and tastes. The higher up the social ladder people stand, the more married they are.

Smoking habits follow the inverse pattern: only one in three university graduates is a smoker, while two out of three less-educated Swedes are nicotine addicts.

As for art, elderly boardroom directors and middle-aged labourers share a passion for the Swedish realist painters Anders Zorn and Bruno Liljefors, except that the former prefer originals purely for investment purposes while the latter settle for reproductions just to please the eye. The more sedate middle class favours prints of Carl Larsson's art nouveau interiors.

Wealth and Fame

Becoming rich in Sweden has never been easy. As Ingmar Bergman found out, even millionaires can have difficulties making ends meet when income tax is levied at 102%.

But even after taxation, the filthy-rich remain merely filthy in the eyes of the not-so-rich, who themselves are far from poor. Manifestations of personal wealth have always been frowned upon in Sweden, based on the assumption that for every winner there has to be a loser.

The only greater sin than being rich is being famous. It is acceptable to acquire fame that rubs off on Sweden as a whole, allowing everyone to bask in the limelight. The fame of Ingemar Stenmark and Pernilla Wiberg is tolerated because it has put Swedish skiing on the map. Ingmar Bergman is allowed to be famous because his films bare the Swedish body and soul to the world.

But Ingrid Bergman, glamorous star of such Hollywood classics as *Casablanca* and *Indiscreet*, fell foul of her Swedish audiences because she earned her fame as an expatriate and failed to flaunt her Swedish origins at every opportunity.

Money Matters

The Swedes truly understand the joy of giving and taking. They give as much as they take, neither more nor less. In kind, or in *kronor* and *öre*. To the second decimal, generously rounded up from the third. Offer a Swedish smoker a cigarette, and he will insist on paying for it. He knows the price of a pack by heart, divides it by 20 in his head, balances 1 *krona* 99½ *öre* on the tip of his tongue, and counts out 2 *kronor* in the palm of his hand. "Here," he will say to the donor, "and keep the change."

Restaurant bills are divided up among friends after a meal, not just divided into equal shares, but everyone remembers exactly what he ordered and does his own calculation on the paper napkin. Ulf and Ulla out on a date are equally intent on settling their score evenly.

A foreign observer of scenes like these could be forgiven for thinking that the Swedes are pathological skinflints.

The truth, however, is that they loathe becoming dependent on other human beings through indebtedness in any shape or form. Accept a gift and one feels obliged to reciprocate in kind. Receive a favour, and count on it being called in at a later date.

An assistant professor at Lund University was appalled by this tit-for-tat mania when he arrived in Sweden as a refugee from Chile. He describes encountering a Swedish colleague at a language course in England.

He decided to attempt some cultural engineering. "Let's make a deal," he suggested. "In Sweden we've always done it your way and split the bill, but as long as we're here in England let's do it my way and take turns treating each other. OK?"

The colleague reluctantly agreed. For two months they entertained each other à la chilienne. In fact the refugee professor happened to have more pocket money than his Swedish friend and enjoyed pampering him a little.

On the journey back to Sweden, just as the professor was silently congratulating himself for having weaned his friend off the nasty habit of bill-splitting, the latter cheerfully announced: "By the way, I've been doing the sums of what we spent in those English pubs, and I come out owing you 147 *kronor*."

Religion

There is a saying that all Swedish people are born free but taxed to death. In fact, until 1996, all children were born into the Lutheran faith – the doctrine of the Church of Sweden – whether they liked it or not. Those who have not opted out show their Lutheran piety by attending church on at least four occasions, namely for their baptism, confirmation, wedding(s) and funeral.

In an effort to meet the spiritual needs of the increasingly pagan population, the clergy are becoming inventive. Nowadays married couples may receive the blessing of the Church not only at the wedding ceremony, but also before an impending divorce. The ritual takes the form of a prayer for forgiveness, during which the couple can thank each other for the good times they spent together.

Another creative touch is the presence of 'prayer bowls' on the tables of popular Stockholm restaurants, allowing diners to write down requests for prayers and deposit them in the bowls. These are later collected by Baptist vicars who mobilise their congregations to relay the prayers to the Lord for further action.

The new translation of the Old Testament commissioned by the Church has been heavily criticised by the Women's Faction of the Leftist Party. Though the translation won praise for its accuracy, they objected to the Testament's blatantly male chauvinist bias. Their tenet is that when God created Man, She was only joking.

The Church of Sweden is still struggling with its list of priorities. For instance, it is all right for the clergy to doubt the existence of God but according to a Synod recommendation no-one may be ordained as a pastor who does not accept woman pastors.

The presence of God in Sweden may be in doubt, but there is an omnipotent Force in whom everybody firmly believes, the Force that screws everything up – or at least is blamed for it. Ask a Swedish builder about the defects in his latest luxury condominium, and he will reply: "Well, mistakes certainly seem to have crept into the construction."

Behaviour

Women and Men

To the foreign eye, Sweden appears to be inhabited by two radically different tribes: the Women and the Men.

The stereotype Swedish Woman is beautiful, opinionated and speaks three languages. She has a strong aesthetic sense and her attitude to sex is accommodating. While single, she travels the world and samples the local climatic and climactic delights. Once married, she invariably has a career and keeps her own money.

The average Swedish Man is seen as being shy, taciturn, submissive, sentimental, principled, reliable – precisely the sort of male companion the Swedish woman covets as the father of her 1¾ children. He is Mr. Fixit who also knows how to push a pram and change a baby. He is basically a loner and is happiest at work, on the ski slope or at the country cottage which he is constantly rebuilding.

Swedes congratulate themselves for having been first in the world to achieve total equality between the sexes. They base this statistic on the fact that about half of the government ministers are female, as are almost half the Members of Parliament. In the public sector, 70% of staff are women – but 60% of their bosses are men.

By international standards, Swedish women have always been highly emancipated. In the days of the Vikings, only a woman dared tell a warrior what a corny oaf he was. If another man ventured a similar observation, it usually cost him one or more extremities. Nowadays members of the Women's Movement are campaigning for men to sit down when urinating, their point being that men have been flaunting their anatomical advantage for much too long.

One thing Swedish men and women do have in common is a curious diagnostic attitude to human relationships.

Social, as well as sexual, intercourse techniques are analysed and compared in great detail – along the lines of "How was it for you?", and "How can we improve it next time?". To a foreigner, this rather clinical approach can be unsettling, but it does provide a head start in later encounters.

Marriage

Since the Middle Ages, the Swedish Church has faithfully recorded births, marriages and deaths on behalf of the secular authorities. In the absence of major wars on home turf, the old ledgers remain intact and constitute the most complete record of human lineage in the world. American Mormons of Swedish extraction have been particularly active in tracing their ancestry to convert their forebears retroactively.

The fact that half of the adult population in Sweden lives alone, and that couples are usually not married, does not deter traditionalists and incurable romantics from giving marriage a try. Those who do get married often include their offspring in their wedding photos.

After a decade of studied simplicity, weddings have once more become elaborate rituals. Church weddings have made a comeback, and the most picturesque churches are booked up months in advance. The groom himself, rather than the father-in-law, leads the bride to the altar, usually to the tune of Mendelssohn's Wedding March (which happens to be the traditional exit march in America, causing American wedding guests to think they've come too late for the ceremony).

The groom is usually dressed in black tails, while the bride's gown is ivory white with coloured flowers sewn onto the hem and wild meadow flowers adorn her hair. Even in times of deep recession, most couples splurge on designer gold rings, sumptuous receptions and luxurious honeymoons.

The modern Swedish marriage is based on a formula involving mutual respect and independence. The success of this formula may be judged by the divorce rate which is over 50%.

The traditional role models within the marriage began to disintegrate in the 1960s when wives called for financial independence from their husbands and demanded monthly *hustrulön*, or wife salary. The claim was justified on the grounds that the wife was in effect a housekeeper and a nanny rolled into one (though most husbands would probably have preferred rolling with each separately). Paradoxically, the *hustrulön* offered husbands a financial incentive since, having previously handed all their earnings to their wives, they now only had to part with two-thirds. *Hustrulön* became the norm in Swedish marriages until wives eventually gained complete financial independence through job careers of their own.

Alas, with independent salaries came an added tax burden. The suggestion has been made that spouses formally employ each other as household contractors to obtain certain corporate tax exemptions. This would clearly be a win-win situation: one spouse makes money around the clock while the other deducts the marital charges from the income tax. For instance, a wife's invoice to her husband for a typical day of married bliss might look like this:

Services rendered	*Kronor*
Wake-up call	40
Finding matching socks	100
Making breakfast	150
Getting 1¾ children ready for school	200
Preparing supper	600
Helping 1¾ children with homework	300
Escort duties out on the town	1,000

20

Going Dutch on nightclub and taxi charges	1,800
Sex	N/C
Kinky sex supplement	400
Post-coital advice	150
Management fee	300
Subtotal	5,040
VAT 25%	1,260
Grand total	6,300

Children

The statutory maternity leave is 12 months at 80% of the mother's most recent salary, plus another 3 months at a reduced rate. Since nearly all couples have parallel careers, it is up to the mother and the father to decide who stays at home with the newborn child. As a result, Swedish men excel in breast feeding and changing nappies. If the mother wants to return to work earlier, she may use her remaining maternity leave at her leisure until the child's eighth birthday.

While a Mediterranean mother might smack her child one minute and console it with hugs and kisses the next, Swedish parents abhor inconsistency in the upbringing of their offspring. For starters, spanking a child – even one's own – is against the law in Sweden. Deprived of unambiguous correctional remedies, Swedish parents allow their children to sprout without much pruning, but day-care centres, and later the schools, catch these untamed little savages and turn them into highly indepen-dent adolescents.

The Elderly

In the days of the Vikings, the worst dishonour, next to cowardice, that could befall a warrior was to survive every battle only to die in bed of old age. If he was fortunate enough to have two sons, however, he could save his honour by having them push him over the edge of a cliff. The cliff was known as an *ättestupa*, or Ancestral Precipice.

Today the elderly are treated more sympathetically. Even so, the low birth rate coupled with the high life expectancy (82 for women, 77 for men) makes for a top-heavy society with many wrinkles, one of which is the pension system.

Whoever promised Swedish pensioners 60% of their highest salary must either have been a poor mathematician or else held a grudge against posterity which is now having to foot the bill. The growing population of pensioners is being supported by a steadily shrinking workforce so the Ancestral Precipice may soon become popular again.

Immigrants

In the last 100 years, Sweden has gone from being a country of emigrants to becoming a haven for immigrants. The drab warp of the ethnic fabric has been inextricably blended with more exotic weft from the farthest corners of the globe. One inhabitant in eight is either a naturalised foreigner or a refugee.

There are the inevitable cranks who complain that the immigrants take all the good jobs and the best apartments, but most Swedish citizens show a degree of tolerance towards the newcomers. One reason for this is that Swedish supermarkets and restaurants have been compelled to widen the food selection beyond gruel and fermented herring. Another reason is that the incomers provide folklore entertainment previously only available on expensive charter trips.

The immigrants enjoy complaining about Sweden – its climate, taxes and indigenous population – and say they can hardly wait to leave. The Swedes find this attitude coming from foreigners rather uncharitable. But when the Swedes themselves voice exactly the same complaints, everyone nods in full agreement.

Animals

In Sweden the horses say *"gnägg-gnägg"* (gneg-gneg) and the pigs say *"nöff-nöff"* (nuff-nuff). How they communicate with their counterparts in other countries is a mystery.

The Swedes don't dote on their animals to the same degree as, for instance, British rat fanciers or German tropical snake collectors, nor do they grow to resemble their pets. Animals in Sweden fulfil both a victual and a social function, but an instinct for self-preservation keeps the Swedes from emulating them. Wandering the forests looking morose like a moose is certain to get you shot during the hunting season. Swedish hunters fire at anything on four legs, including pairs of mushroom pickers walking in tandem.

In Sweden, therefore, the onus of emulation is on the animals themselves, the dogs generally imitating the men while the cats take after the women. As the Swedish saying goes: 'Like master, like dog'. The dogs have done particularly well and are now paying taxes like everybody else.

Driving

Even the most exasperated Swedish driver will normally yield to buses trying to pull out, and will let old ladies reach the other side of the street before revving the engine. But from time to time these emotional icicles do experience a thaw behind the wheel – twice a week, to be precise. On Friday afternoons at 4 o'clock sharp they leave their desks, jump into their Volvos and Saabs, and weave their way through the rush-hour traffic with uncharacteristic pitilessness. Once home, they pack two pairs of everything, put food in the cooler bag, water the flowers, set the video timer, change the answerphone message, lock the front door three times and launch themselves into a traffic mêlée which makes Fifth Avenue look like a village high street. This is the moment when the Svenssons set out for their country cottages to get some rest.

The pattern is repeated in reverse on Sunday nights. More Swedish adrenaline flows in the course of these two-hour pilgrimages to Mother Nature than during the entire working week.

Manners

Queuing

Visitors are often surprised that there are no queues in Sweden. In banks, post offices, pharmacies and bakeries people with expressionless faces wander around aimlessly as if trying to remember where they are. From time to time a loud buzz is transmitted from a box under the ceiling. The buzz has the effect of jogging the memory of one of the customers and launching him towards one of the service counters.

The box under the ceiling is in fact a numeric display which changes with every buzz. The change is triggered when a clerk presses an electric button, prompting each customer to compare the new number with a kind of lottery ticket in his hand. The winner is the next to be served.

In Sweden, unlike in other countries, strangers who head straight from the entrance to the counter risk neither insult nor injury from waiting customers. Without a lottery ticket, the stranger simply will not be served by the clerk. The real challenge is to find the ticket dispenser which is usually cleverly hidden behind a pillar, a notice board or an urn with man-eating plants. Finding the dispenser is a national sport; a stranger asking for clues is met with a smug grin and a toss of the head, usually in the wrong direction.

Greetings

The informal Swedish greeting *tjänare* (literally 'servant') is supposed to mean 'I am your humble servant', but the accompanying vigorous handshake and slap on the back abruptly dispel the impression of servitude.

When the Swedes greet each other, you don't know whether they are coming or going. The most common salutation is *hej* which is used both as a greeting and as a farewell. The Swedes think the English translation of *hej* is "Hi!"; so when a departing Swedish woman bids "Hi!" to her foreign lover after a night of bliss, the latter suffers heart fibrillations thinking she wants to start all over again.

Hospitality

The Swedes behave as if no honour could be greater than playing host to a foreign visitor. When they come to visit you in your country, you are obviously the host. They will hold forth about how expensive everything is in Sweden until your natural hospitality becomes mingled with guilt, so you wine and dine them more lavishly than you had perhaps intended. You may even invite them to stay in your home. No doubt they will graciously accept and will stay for however long it takes to do your honour justice, which could be anything from three weeks to six months.

When the time comes for you to visit them in Sweden and be pampered in return, you may be in for a surprise, for your friends are likely to receive you with a welcome dinner at your hotel. At your expense. They reason that if you can afford a Swedish hotel, you must be travelling on an expense account, so why deprive you of the honour of playing host once more?

If you feel strongly about role reversal, you may wish to show up unannounced on your friends' doorstep with a heavy suitcase in each hand. They will of course feel honour-bound to accommodate you in their home. You will be given a choice of bunk beds in the children's nursery as well as useful hints on how to catch a bus downtown. They wouldn't, however, dream of sending you off on an empty stomach. Your first meal will probably be something special, such as raw fish, over which your hosts will regale you with germane Swedish sayings along the lines that 'fish and guests smell bad after three days'. Then they will enquire about your date of departure.

The Swedish brand of hospitality may appear to others to be ungenerous. It is true that in most Western cultures there is a tacit understanding that the guest/host relationship should be a two-way street. But while the rest of us deck out the street with elaborate garlands of false pretences ("Do come and see us anytime!" or "Surely you're not leaving us so soon?"), the Swedes stake out the limits of their hospitality in no uncertain terms. They assume that you will do the same. So when you tell them to come and see you anytime, they will do precisely that. And if you protest that they're leaving much too soon, they'll stay on to keep you company. It's a square, square world.

Conversation

The Taboo Subject

The Swedes consider themselves the most broad-minded people on earth. They boast that only in Sweden are you free to discuss absolutely anything, be it sex, money, incest or euthanasia. Don't take their word for it, though, because generalising about nationalities (other than Norwegians) is definitely out.

Swedish people love to criticise their own country when amongst themselves; but when a foreigner enters the room, suddenly Sweden can do nothing wrong. They particularly dislike foreigners attempting Swedish jokes. Try the following riddle at a Swedish party:

Q: What do vegetarian cannibals eat?
A: Swedes.

Rest assured, you'll never be invited back.

Body Language

Linguists, social anthropologists and pornographers agree that body language makes up 80% of communication between humans. For all their foreign language skills, Swedes don't have any body language, which means that 80% of the communication is lost on them; hence the "Huh?" syndrome. Academics from abroad lecturing at Swedish universities complain that, in the absence of body language, they have absolutely no idea whether the students have absorbed even the remaining 20%. The only time the average Swede uses body language spontaneously is when he flails his arms to drive away wasps from his summer picnic.

A peculiar Swedish preoccupation is what to do with one's hands. At dinner table it used to be popular to keep them busy with a cigarette or twirling the stem of a wine glass but, with smoking and drinking having gone out of fashion, Swedish hands are once more looking for adventure. It is precisely for this reason that young people are taught to keep their hands clearly visible on top of the table.

Conference junkies are sent to public speaking seminars partly to learn what to do with their limbs. Crossing one's arms is out (too defensive), as is standing with arms akimbo (too aggressive) or concealing one's hands in trouser pockets (too suggestive). Those who finally get the picture accompany their discourse with incongruous contortions more often seen in Indonesian dance.

Forms of Address

The Swedish language, like most non-English languages, allows the speaker to determine social distance by using the polite form *Ni* or the informal *Du*. As people began buying cars and traffic collisions became commonplace, '*Ni*' accompanied by a wagging finger was the primary means of trading insults. The formerly polite pronoun gradually developed an aggressive connotation and was shunned throughout the 1950s and 60s.

But people still had to talk to each other, even at arm's length. This was cunningly arranged by addressing each other in the third person or seeking refuge in convoluted passive syntax. For instance, the question: "Aren't you going to Acapulco this year?" became: "Is it to be not going to Acapulco this year?" (which was likely to yield the answer: "No, that was last year. This year we're not going to Hawaii.")

By 1970 the Swedes had had enough of this syntactic self-torture and, riding on the new egalitarian wave, began to use '*Du*' with just anybody. But the older citizens never got used to this instant chumminess and treated '*Du*' users with disdain. In the late 80s, as enthusiasm for egalitarianism subsided, '*Ni*' began to make a comeback, purified by the passage of time and a decrease in the number of traffic accidents.

Swearwords

At a formal Swedish Embassy dinner, a Canadian wife sitting next to her Swedish husband was asked whether she spoke any Swedish. "Oh yes, I pick it up from my husband," she replied cheerfully, "*satans djävlar i helvete*!" The ambassador choked on his champagne and the dinner conversation ground to a gasping halt. Yet all she had said was 'Satan's little devils in Hell'.

Given the agnostic disposition of Swedish people, it may come as a surprise that the most potent Swedish swearwords involve Heaven and Hell rather than scatological or anatomical epithets. The Swedes remain convinced that things go wrong only when demons from the Underworld decide to interfere; calling out their identities is a tried and tested Lutheran method of dispatching them back to Purgatory.

Eating and Drinking

Swedish Cuisine

Ask any foreigner what he or she knows about Sweden, and the answer will be along the lines of Björn Borg, Volvo, Saab, Ikea, watches, and raw fish. Unfortunately, Borg has emigrated to Monaco, while Volvo and Saab have been taken over by American auto giants Ford and General Motors. Ikea has moved its headquarters to

Denmark and watches are made in Switzerland, not Sweden. So that leaves raw fish.

This arrives on the table in the form of pickled Baltic herring and is the centrepiece on the Swedish *smörgås-bord*, a unique gluttony gala where seafoods, salads, cold cuts and cheeses vie for the attention of gourmands. In addition one can usually find delectable meatballs and a concoction of anchovies and scalloped potatoes called *Janssons frestelse*, or Jansson's Temptation.

Foreign visitors enjoying buffet breakfasts in Swedish hotels are often dismayed to discover pickled herring next to the cornflakes. People for whom breakfast is a celebration of carbohydrates and cholesterol spurn flaccid fish fillets floating belly-up in vinegar. For their part the Swedes blanch as Orientals sprinkle salt on their grapefruit or as North Americans pour maple syrup over their bacon, so raw fish should not be sniffed at.

There is, however, a special Swedish herring recipe which makes foreigners not only sniff but positively asphyxiate. It is called *surströmming*.

A Swedish freighter in San Francisco was stranded in port because the American half of the crew had walked off the ship and refused to return. Interviewed by the local newspapers, crew members described how the Swedish chef served 'rotten fish' which was so vile that the portholes steamed up and the paint flaked off the walls. The label 'rotten fish' shows a typical foreign lack of appreciation of *surströmming*, a time-honoured Swedish delicacy.

The recipe is simple enough. Fresh herring fillets are sealed in sardine tins where they undergo a fermentation process for a few months. Under pressure of the swelling fish, the tins begin to bulge. Once they have adopted the shape of an American football, the tins are opened using a technique developed for the controlled detonation of terrorist bombs. The fillets are extracted at arm's length, rolled into thin slabs of potato-flour bread, ingested, and washed down with a gulp of aquavit. The American crew simply made the mistake of not holding their breath for 30 minutes.

The most widely consumed bread is *knäckebröd,* which looks like rectangular pieces of thin brown fibreboard and tastes like unprocessed cellulose. Known elsewhere as crispbread, most foreign clones are based on the original Swedish recipe – so brittle that it shatters if buttered on a sideplate; hence the Swedish habit of holding it for spreading.

Anyone wondering what really makes the Swedes tick need look no further: it is coffee. A coffee embargo would bring the country to a halt within days. Coffee is the only reason for waking up in the morning and is the just reward after each chore during the day. Dinner without coffee would be unthinkable.

A Swedish coffee party is a noisy affair, a reckless feast of extortionately expensive bakery delectables. The cakes are covered with green marzipan, or sliced almonds ('toe-nails'), while the pastries have gobs of vanilla and strawberry jam in the middle ('grandmother's cough'). Dunking biscuits in the coffee is considered bad manners but is done anyway, with apologies; pieces that fall in are systematically tracked down and rescued with a spoon.

Drinking

It is often said that the Swedes have a drinking problem. This sweeping generalisation seems to stem from observations that Swedish pedestrians frequently cling to lamp-posts, and that Swedish package tour travellers occasionally have to be disembarked on stretchers. However such testimony would hardly stand up in court as proof of national drunkenness. As a matter of official fact, Swedes consume less alcohol than most other nations within the European Union (less than 5 litres per annum, in terms of pure alcohol, compared with more than 11 litres in France and Portugal).

The most effective deterrent against alcohol consumption in Sweden is the state monopoly of its sale. In the paternalistic belief that it is helping the Swedes to control their alcohol intake, the Swedish government is defying E.U. law by restricting the sale of spirits. Outlets are few and far between, open late, close early, demand personal identification and mask the whereabouts of liquor by displaying everything but spirits in their windows. Citizens who do manage to find one are charged exorbitant prices for anything stronger than wine.

Another deterrent is the stiff penalty meted out to anyone caught driving a vehicle with even a molecule of alcohol in the blood. One hapless driver, who was pulled over and breathalysed seconds after swallowing a rumfilled chocolate, tested positive and was driven away to a police laboratory for blood tests. The tests showed no trace of alcohol and the driver was acquitted, but only after agreeing to pay for the tests as well as a fine for wasting police time.

It would thus be tempting to conclude that the Swedish reputation for excessive drinking is unfounded. But here again the Swedes confound us. Successive temperance-inspired governments have fostered a curious binary attitude to alcohol among the Swedes, i.e. drinking is either good or evil, right or wrong; there can be no middle ground. Hence a large proportion of Sweden's population consumes no spirits at all, while the very audible and visible remainder holds the firm view that the cork, once pulled, must never see the bottle again.

The Mandatory After-Dinner Speech

The exorbitant cost of restaurant meals forces Swedish people without expense accounts to do most of their entertaining at home. However there is no such thing as a simple get-together for an evening snack. The hosts spend all day cooking and cleaning, and at precisely the appointed time the doorbell rings. The guests are lined up on the doorstep, some having driven around the block five times because they were early, others arriving by taxi to avoid the risk of being arrested for drunken driving on the way home. Everybody carries a present. Those who bring flowers unwrap them before handing them to the hostess, discreetly tossing the wrapping paper to the host for disposal.

When arranging the seating around the dinner table, the host employs higher mathematics to ensure that women and men alternate, that no-one is placed either beside or opposite their other half, and that the hosts themselves end up at the opposite short ends of the table. If more than seven guests have been invited, the person who finds himself seated next to the hostess becomes the *hedersgäst*, or guest of honour.

This is the seat every male guest fears because of the social obligations that come with the role. For here is the rule that knows no exceptions: the *hedersgäst* must make a thank-you speech on behalf of the other guests some-time between the main course and the dessert. Not just any old speech, but a humorous one. So while the other guests merrily dig into their soup, hors-d'oeuvre and entrée, the *hedersgäst* plunges himself into deep *svårmod* and loses his appetite while fretting over his speech. In the end he usually earns vigorous applause for his trouble and can at least look forward to the dessert. Even so, accidents happen, as in the case of a particularly nervous speaker who got it all backwards when he stammered: "Our hostess m-m-may not cook like a cook, b-b-but she certainly looks like one!"

Skål!

Even the simple matter of quenching your thirst becomes enormously complicated at Swedish dinner parties, especially if you are a woman. The first glass to be raised must be that of the host as he stands up to wish everybody welcome. Then each lady, or *bordsdam,* has to wait for her *bordskavaljer,* i.e. the gentleman seated on her left, to raise his glass, stare deep into her eyes and exclaim *Skål!* Even after all this, a woman should only drink when one of the gentlemen around the table invites her to do so by saying *skål.*

The exception is the hostess who may *skål* anybody at her leisure yet must never be *skål*-ed herself. But rules are meant to be broken, and if a *bordsdam* decides to drink alone, she is silently informing her *bords-kavaljer* that he is neglecting her. Similarly, if another male guest preempts the *bordskavaljer* by offering the first toast to his *bordsdam,* it is a clear insult and an invitation to rivalry between the two men. The games Swedish people play with *skål* know no limits. Achieving Grandmaster status in chess is easy by comparison.

Etiquette

Another important custom is for the hostess to prepare slightly more food than the guests are likely to consume. This is because it is considered bad style for any guest to take the very last piece of canapé, fillet, cake or whatever. Something must always be left on the serving platter.

On one occasion the hostess had prepared a particularly mouth-watering recipe of Swedish meatballs. When the serving platter had made the rounds among the guests, one meatball remained. The hostess tried to persuade her guests to go for it, but although all six of them were sorely tempted, they dutifully declined.

Meanwhile the host was standing at a sidetable preparing to pour batter into the electric waffle iron for dessert. As he plugged in the appliance the fuse blew, plunging the dining room into total darkness. The ensuing silence was suddenly pierced by a bloodcurdling scream. After the host managed to reset the fuse and the lights came on again, one of the guests was seen holding the last meatball on the end of his fork. Deeply embedded in his extended forearm were five additional forks.

Obsessions

Nature

A great deal of emotion is associated with childhood memories of summers gone by. It has to do with the taste of wild strawberries and the smell of freshly cut hay, listening in bed to the cuckoo at dawn, catching crabs with fish heads on a string, and watching the fishermen tar their hulls.

The Swedes are the world's greatest nature lovers and will spout about it until the cows come home.

There are the endless forests in which families gather mushrooms and pick berries while fighting off swarms of native mosquitoes. Loners like to paddle their canoes along the 100,000 pristine lakes sterilised by acid rain from Britain, and outdoorsy types go cross-country skiing in the mountains of Lapland where the silence is so complete that one can hear the innermost thoughts of one's companion – a mitigating factor in many Swedish murder trials.

The Stockholm archipelago with its 25,000 largely uninhabited islands is the ultimate experience for those obsessed with nature. Throughout the summer, tens of thousands of motor yachts and sailing boats compete for the narrowest sounds, the lushest creeks and the baldest rocks. Here children play Robinson Crusoe while their parents play Childless Couple. The bigger islands with their apple trees and poisonous snakes inspire youngsters to re-enact the Old Testament. And everyone soaks up the sun until it is completely drained and collapses behind the horizon for another six months.

As winter arrives and the sea freezes over, the mainland tourists abandon the islands to a resident core of 6,000 hardy archipelagians. A tourist once asked a group of islanders how they went about combating boredom out there among the skerries. "Well," replied one of the islanders, "in the summer we breed and we fish. But in the winter we can't fish."

Ecology

The Swedes have a dream: to save Nature from Man. This is more than just a vision – it's as close to a passion as the Swedes ever get.

Magazines which once devoted coverage to the conquest of space now report almost exclusively on recycling. In academic and industrial laboratories, scientists turn agricultural waste into food wrapping. A Swedish inventor has come up with a combustion engine which runs on refuse yet refuses to run. And in the marble halls of Parliament, politicians talk more rubbish than ever.

The mantra of Swedish ecologists is: 'We don't own the earth – we have borrowed it from our children.' Sweden has armed itself with sophisticated seismic and radiation sensors to monitor ecological misdemeanours abroad. Hence they were the first in the West to detect the 1986 nuclear disaster at Chernobyl, and to sound the alarm worldwide.

Having milked most domestic rivers for their hydro-electric power potential, the government embarked on an ambitious nuclear reactor construction programme. But the accidents at Chernobyl and Three Mile Island provoked a change of heart, and a referendum resulted in a vote to close all the reactors 'at the earliest convenience'. However, the moment of 'convenience' keeps slipping ever further into the future due to the disappointing output from solar and wind power generators, coupled with stiff legislation against emissions from hydrocarbon fuels. So much for adherence to *vox populi*.

Manufacturers of pre-packaged merchandise do not waste ink on extolling the virtues of the contents. Swedish consumers are more impressed by assurances that the ink is biodegradable and that the box is made from recycled cardboard. Similarly, covers of recent Swedish paperbacks (often found in the guest toilet) certify that the paper has been produced from pure pulp without the addition of chlorine or any other environmentally hazardous substances. This helps to allay any dread of hands-on contamination.

Sense of Humour

Two Swedish gentlemen are having lunch in a restaurant. One of them nods his head in the direction of a man sitting alone at another table.

"Isn't that Fingal Olsson sitting over there?"
"No, he's dead."
"But ... I saw him stir just now!"

Incredible as it may seem, the comedian Martin Ljung had the whole Swedish nation writhing on the floor with laughter as he went on stage and television to repeat this joke over and over, placing the emphasis on a different word each time.

Where other nationalities see humour in outrage or ambiguity, Swedes crack up at the absurd. For instance, they find it hilariously funny that foreigners think they lack a sense of humour.

The Swedes simply love poking fun at the Norwegians. The story goes that the Swedish police were looking for a criminal who was thought to have fled to Norway. They demanded his arrest and extradition from their Norwegian colleagues and furnished them with mugshots taken from the left, the right, and straight on. After a couple of days the Oslo police telephoned and reported: "We have arrested the man to the left and the man to the right. Now we're just looking for the man in the middle."

The fact that the exact same joke is told in Norway about the Swedes underscores the contagious nature of Swedish humour.

Leisure and Pleasure

The Swedes indulge in sport for leisure and sex for pleasure. Some people treat sex as a sport in order to combine leisure with pleasure, and thus save time and energy.

Sport

By the time Björn Borg left world tennis in 1983, a wave of Borgomania inspired every local authority in Sweden to build lavish indoor and outdoor tennis facilities which produced champions such as Wilander, Edberg and Järryd. Swedish top seeds continue to germinate like dandelions on tennis lawns around the world.

Stenmark has similarly inspired Sweden's victories on international ski slopes. The greatest annual ski event in Sweden is the *Vasaloppet*, a 10,000-strong cross-country marathon which winds its way along a 53-mile trek from Sälen to Mora. The role model for this event is Gustav Vasa, the founder of the Swedish State, who got on his skis in the Middle Ages to recruit farmers between Sälen and Mora for a march on Stockholm to overthrow the foreign-dominated government. The farmers, having put their crops to bed for the winter, thought the idea was a lark and happily went to work skewering the country's rulers with their pitchforks.

Bicycling is almost as popular as recycling, with enthusiasts of all ages taking part in the annual 180-mile race around the scenic Lake Vättern. A common summer sight is husband and wife and their $1\frac{3}{4}$ children pedalling along wearing crash helmets and little else, like a formation of contented extraterrestrials.

The Swedes are world champions in orienteering, a form of philately where the participants, armed with compasses and ordnance maps, jog all day through endless forests in search of control stations to have their passbooks stamped. They are expert pathfinders: in post offices and wine shops they are the first to find the queue-eliminating ticket dispenser.

In winter some Swedes make a contest out of running naked from hot saunas to roll around in the snow before heading back into their steaming sanctuary. The bravest jump into holes in the ice. Paradoxically, the cold actually causes a burning sensation for the first 30 seconds; after that, the sensation dwindles to a black-framed obituary in the next day's newspaper.

Moose-hunting is an initiation sport which is supposed to turn little boys into men but, more often, excessive alcohol consumption turns the men into gun-toting little boys. With shots being fired at anything that moves, the wise moose stand absolutely still and watch with amazement. Many years ago the rapid decrease of the Swedish moose population was causing concern. In the winter, moose would sometimes set out across the ice of the

Baltic Sea to visit relatives in Finland, only to find themselves cut off on all sides by icebreakers. The Navy would send out helicopters to drop feed onto the ice floes or, if necessary, lift the marooned animals ashore. The moose showed their gratitude by proliferating to the point where they became a serious road hazard.

But rather than simply machine-gunning the moose, the Swedes came up with a solution which, once again, has all the hallmarks of *lagom*. Moose don't like wolves, and they particularly detest the smell of wolf's urine. The road safety people speculated that moose might be kept off the highways if the ditches were suitably sprayed.

Unfortunately there are few wolves left in Sweden, and only a handful responded to an appeal for urine samples, so Swedish scientists set about developing a synthetic urine. The liquid was kept in vials which were suspended from trees along the roadside, and a single charge was supposed to be enough to keep the moose at bay for nine months. The experiment didn't work. Swedish moose aren't stupid; they know that the wolves are virtually extinct, and that those remaining do not climb trees to relieve themselves. So now the war is on, with hunters killing tens of thousands of moose every year, and the animals using kamikaze tactics to take revenge on white-knuckled road users.

Sex

President Eisenhower once noted in a speech that there was a country in Northern Europe where moral standards had fallen to an all-time low. The subsequent avalanche of American tourists upon Swedish soil left little doubt which country he had in mind. The visitors were not disappointed for they returned home with photographic evidence that Swedish people swim naked whenever they think nobody is watching. The interest in sex stretches far beyond Homo Sapiens. In the 18th century, Linnaeus studied the sex life of plants with such intensity that he became known as the Peeping Tom of Botany.

Surprisingly Swedes do take time off from having sex, e.g. when consuming fermented herring. It is true, however, that their attitude to sex is largely unencumbered by taboos. The Swedes, like the Dutch, believe in easy natural sex as a way of resisting unnatural forms such as prostitution, incest and child abuse.

The only mystery surrounding Swedish sex is why they make it so uncomfortable. Double beds are a rarity in Sweden. Single beds with sharp wooden edges are the norm in hotels, and in youth hostels bunk beds have paper sheets that rustle.

Health and Hygiene

Swedish people dislike their natural blond pallor – they see it as a sign of ill health. In the spring when the sun comes out and the temperature rises above freezing, the Swedes emerge from their work places, apartments and country houses to lay the foundation for their annual sun tan. In towns, shoppers and office workers jockey for position on park benches and at bus stops to steal a share of the timid sunlight. In the countryside, white faces turn like sunflowers to track the sun across the sky.

In the summer, weather permitting, people head for the coastline and strip bare to bathe in sunlight and water. With the arrival of autumn, the rapidly falling temperature drives the sun worshippers into saunas where tanned bottoms distinguish those who spent their holidays in Sweden from the white bottoms of those who went abroad.

Following cutbacks in sick leave benefits by a right-wing government, Swedes miraculously became much healthier. So while other governments buckle under the ever increasing cost of keeping the population healthy, the Swedes have figured out that health can be restored by cutting costs. The left-wingers subsequently ousted those right-wingers by promising a re-instatement of the old sick leave benefits. As a result, sick leave is now making a massive comeback.

Hygiene

Most modern Swedish hotels only provide showers for guests, and older hotels are stripping out their original wonderfully deep bathtubs.

In their homes, Swedes prefer showers to bathtubs because they take less time, consume less water, are more hygienic, and offer more intimate acoustics for arias.

Foreigners visiting Swedish homes are often mildly shocked to discover a bag of sanitary towels hanging from a peg in the W.C. According to Swedish logic, if you are going to hide the sanitary towels, you might as well hide the lavatory paper too. The latter is highly recycled and is reminiscent of Grade 60 sandpaper.

Culture

Literature and Drama

Intellectual arrogance is alien to the Swedes, for whom the Truth is attained empirically rather than analytically. For example, you may not be able to define pornography, but you certainly recognise it when you see it.

Swedish fiction concerns itself with what can be seen, heard, smelled, tasted and touched. It aspires to be Deep and Meaningful without trying to solve the Mystery of Life. Many contemporary Swedish writers favour a phantasmagoric medley of experimental logic and excremental smut which is so deep and meaningful that no critic, let alone reader, dares to criticise it for fear of being thought shallow.

A few leading lights have managed to rise above the literary fog to the point of receiving international attention. One was the author and playwright August Strindberg who turned 19th-century morality upside down by castigating accepted norms and values, notably marriage and patriotism. Another was Selma Lagerlöf whose farmhand character Nils Holgersson made aviation history by flying all over Sweden on the back of a goose.

Among Sweden's 20th-century writers, Vilhelm Moberg and Sven Delblanc move their plots forward and often place their characters in a cosmopolitan setting. Both have painted compelling portraits of Swedish immigrants in North America – not the brawny cowboy or golddigger types fabricated in Hollywood, but simple farmers who gave up what little they owned in exchange for even less. Most of the other contemporary novelists cater to a peculiarly Swedish taste for flawed characters engaged in bizarre activities and relationships.

Sweden's biggest literary hit abroad is perhaps Astrid Lindgren's brainchild *Pippi Longstocking*, a strapping freckled brat with intractable braids who lives alone with her horse and her monkey in a ramshackle mansion while her father, a sea captain, is away. With nobody to supervise her, she breaks every rule of polite behaviour, to the joy of the other children in the village and to the horror of their parents. Her house is a mess. When she makes pancakes, half of them have to be scraped off the ceiling.

In short, Pippi is the last glimpse of barefoot abandon a Swedish child is allowed to catch before its soul is encapsulated in an Ice Age of *svårmod* and *undfallenhet*.

The Press

Along with Norway, Finland and Japan, Sweden leads the world in the number of people reading newspapers. Most of the newspapers serve as the mouthpiece for a particular political party, and 80% of these support the non-Socialist block. Even so, most governments in the last 100 years have been Socialist, which suggests that Swedes don't believe anything they read.

The leading newspapers are *Dagens Nyheter* and *Aftonbladet,* the former appearing in the morning and the latter in the evening. These two publications set the tone for the rest of the Swedish news media by avoiding substance and concentrating on form. Rather than edifying the readership on the issues at stake in the political, economic and ecological arena, they devote column after column to procedural analysis, negotiation tactics and other forms of political wrangling. Entertainment is limited to sporadic attempts to bring down the government, while wit is relegated to the cartoons.

Newspapers in Sweden are not all bad, however; for only in Sweden are the pages glued or stapled together along the centreline to curtail their annoying habit of falling all over the floor.

One of the most widely read periodicals in Sweden is Walt Disney's *Donald Duck*. On trains and buses, in parks and on beaches, Swedes can be seen reading *Donald Duck* with the same voracity that Russians absorb Pushkin or Tolstoy in public. The national predilection for the jacketed and trouserless duck has so far defied all social theorising.

Television

Swedish television is neither entertaining nor edifying, but to a foreigner it can seem extremely funny, for newsreaders, quiz show hosts, and even newsworthy citizens singled out for interviews always look absolutely terrified.

Every Saturday night, four million people (nearly half the entire population) glue themselves to their TV sets for three hours to watch *Bingo Lotto*. At first glance *Bingo Lotto* is simply conventional bingo by remote control. As numbers are called out on the screen, viewers mark them down on numbered bingo forms which they have bought beforehand. Everyone who gets a winning line receives at least three times the purchase price by sending in the form.

What makes *Bingo Lotto* unusual are the astronomical prizes – worth several million every week – which are given away to winners who manage to phone in and get on the air. The nervous game host asks the petrified caller to pick a box or a painting on display in the studio. After much "Huh?" and "*Nja*" (an elision of *nej* meaning no and *ja* meaning yes), the caller takes his pick and finds himself the winner of a brand new Volvo, a trip around the world for two, or a toaster. As if that wasn't enough, a form-holder can win huge sums following a lucky draw of his form's serial number by filling in additional quiz boxes on the form, or by being at home when his telephone is dialled at random during the show.

There is a very Swedish twist to the game, because most of the loot is paid out in goods and services rather than cash. Consequently toddlers are saddled with honeymoon trips to Hawaii, anti-pollution campaigners with 5,000 litres of petrol, and anorexics with free groceries for a year. The biggest prize winners receive a pile of government bonds which are really lottery tickets in disguise. They rarely produce dividends; but if they do, much of the payout is confiscated through taxes as 'unearned income'.

Cinema

Sweden has a great deal in common with Disney World. On the surface people seem to lead a carefree existence in a fairy-tale paradise. Underneath is a whole different world which is out of bounds for most visitors. In Disney World, this sprawling subterranean facility shelters the machinery that drives the props above ground. In Sweden it conceals what animates the Swedish people – their Swedish Soul.

Gaining access to the Swedish Soul can be difficult. Their navel-gazing literature offers few clues, and the news media even fewer. There is a secret entrance, however, in the form of Swedish cinema. This art form is the precinct not only of Bergman, but of a whole dynasty of talented film makers and actors casting their nets in a sea teeming with Soul and fat government subsidies.

As one breaks through the ice of Swedishness, one discovers a veritable ocean of human feeling ranging from paranoid anguish to unbridled exhilaration, with *svårmod* and *undfallenhet* floating somewhere in the middle. This is not a placid pond but a churning maelstrom; it sucks the spectator into a dizzying journey through situations and relationships which are as plausible as they are bewildering and disturbing. If these are snapshots of Swedish life below the surface, then the Swedes must be forgiven for sometimes looking rather dazed and dispirited. With a Soul like that, who needs a Spirit?

Art and Design

Swedish design is bright, cheerful and indestructible – in other words, the opposite of the Swedish Soul. This makes sense: if the people are saddled with a disposition of dark *svårmod*, the last thing they want is a delicately carved mahogany rocking chair that collapses when they slump into it. *Svårmod* also confers a sense of insecurity, which is why the Volvo automobile is designed like a tank with airbags everywhere.

To keep their *svårmod* at bay, the Swedes surround themselves with eye-pleasing forms, be they decorated roller-blinds, sensuous wineglasses or coloured candles with matching paper napkins. Ikea superstores are the Mecca of Swedish practical design – not just self-assembly furniture, but everything from dishtowels to wall-mounted beer can crushers. The founder, Ingvar Kamprad, started out with a mail-order firm selling Christmas cards to cheer up his countrymen during World War II. Today Kamprad, one of Sweden's wealthiest citizens, can look back on more than 50 years of creative challenge embodied in approximately 150 Ikea superstores in three dozen countries – a feat which he is known to celebrate, not with champagne, but with a glass of chilled aquavit accompanied by new potatoes with dill and a slice of raw herring.

Music

Music is another area where the Scandinavian countries strongly differ. In Finland the martial orchestration of Sibelius' symphonic works captures the heroism of a people repelling successive invasions of Russians, Germans, wolves and mosquitoes. In Norway Grieg extols the virtues of the maiden on the mountaintop who milks her cow while pining for her lover. In Denmark milk curdles to cheese to the sound of Nielsen's polyphonic dissonances. Swedish music is alone in offering the listener mental tranquillity as it evokes no images whatsoever. Here the orchestral winds are reduced to a bronchial concertina, the strings to an offbeat fiddle, and the timpani to clog-clad foot-stomping in three-quarter time.

Sweden is nevertheless the home of some of the world's

most renowned singers, with Jenny Lind, Birgit Nilsson and Abba being the brightest stars in the firmament. Abba have sold 250 million records and began their ascent in the 1970s by winning the Eurovision Song Contest three times. This happy outcome can be explained through the theory of probability rather than music, since the Scandinavian countries usually vote for each other – except for Sweden, which consistently throws its weight behind countries facing *nul points*. (Well, someone has to stick up for the underdog, especially if one aspires to be The World's Conscience.)

Custom and Tradition

Public Holidays

Deep down in the Swedish character there is a bear. Not the ferocious variety with hair on its chest, but the kind that dozes through the winter in a constipated stupor wondering when spring will arrive.

In Sweden, somewhat optimistically, many regard Easter as the first sign of spring. The symbol of the season is the Easter Witch, a hag of unrivalled ugliness. Legend has it that she takes off at sunrise on her flying broom to consort with the Devil at a place named Blåkulla (Blue Hill), a tea-kettle dangling from the front of the broom and a black cat hanging on for dear life at the back. Some say that on the way she barges into children's nurseries and smacks their behinds with her broom before handing out papier-mâché eggs filled with marzipan sweets. Since the law was passed against spanking children, only the sweets are now handed out.

Walpurgis Night on 30th April heralds the official start of spring. During the day, tens of thousands of university students in white caps take to the streets chanting an old song which celebrates their carefree future. This song was composed before the dole queue was invented. At night people gather around bonfires on hilltops across the country to buoy each other up with patriotic speeches.

The Swedish Maypole is legendary, not least because it is erected in June. Midsummer's Day, or rather night, is the time for fun and procreation. Aquavit – the spirit of life – is the aphrodisiac of the season. There is much dancing on the jetty to the accompaniment of whining violins and wheezing accordions. In most countries dancing is a vertical method of satisfying a horizontal need; in Sweden it is just the appetiser.

During August the Swedes look forward to their annual *kräftskiva*, an intimate evening get-together to consume freshwater crayfish. If the weather permits, the party is held outdoors under candle-lit paper lanterns. Part of the fun used to be catching the little crustaceans which, like Swedish tanks, are built for *undfallenhet* and come equipped with two speeds forward and five speeds backward. Today most of the crayfish consumed are imported frozen into Sweden, but frozen or alive, they are unceremoniously thrown into boiling water where they turn lobster red. Their flavour, subtle at best, becomes non-existent as tastebuds are numbed by a steady flow of aquavit.

The best known Swedish celebration is undoubtedly Sancta Lucia, as epitomised by a nubile blonde maiden with burning candles in her hair. In the early hours of the 13th December each year, she and her entourage of young boys and girls wade through the snow wearing slippers, night shirts and not much else. They go from house to house awakening the residents with angelic song, giving out steaming coffee and ginger biscuits.

Like most Swedish public holidays, the celebration of Sancta Lucia has heathen origins and used to be a raucous affair until the 18th century when the Italian

Saint Lucia was co-opted to give it religious respectability.

Before her beatification she was a beautiful maiden. When her admirer told her she had gorgeous eyes, she promptly tore them out and presented them to him on a silver platter. According to the story she quickly grew new eyes and thus found herself strapped to a pole to be burned as a witch. But when the flames refused even to singe her, they had to take her down and decapitate her.

Christmas in Sweden is celebrated on the evening of 24th December. The man of the house disappears for a quick change of clothes and returns in the guise of Santa Claus carrying a sack full of loot. Then, with insight into child psychology, he first frightens the children to death before inundating them with presents. It teaches the little rascals not to take gifts for granted, and scars them for life.

Christmas is also the season for mulled wine. The Swedish variety is served piping hot and is called *glögg* because of the sound it makes when swallowed. Some people prefer a fortified recipe of *glögg* which is potent enough to propel a space rocket. Take four bottles of cheap red wine, add two bottles of pure spirit, mix in orange and lemon peel, sugar, cinnamon sticks, cloves, raisins and almonds, turn off the lights, and set fire to the whole thing. *Glögg* is served by ladling the burning brew into tiny glasses without spilling it into the laps of guests.

The Swedes celebrate the birth of the New Year with all the jollity of a funeral. While the rest of humanity is throwing streamers and wearing funny hats, the Swedish sit transfixed before their television screens watching an actor read solemn poetry. When he is done, the room resounds with the mighty chimes of cathedral bells, counterpointed by popping champagne corks. At precisely midnight the assembled stand up, champagne glass in hand and tears in the eyes, and wish each other a Happy New Year.

Government

Politics

The Swedish political scene has long been dominated by five main parties. Sweden was run more or less continuously from 1932 until 1976 by the Socialists who created the Swedish welfare state. They took from the rich and gave to the poor until everyone was on welfare.

Tired of socialist excesses, the voters chose a conservative coalition known as the 'Bourgeois'. But the new government let down the electorate by simply continuing the welfare programme where the Socialists had left off.

The voters began casting about between the Socialists and the Bourgeois in order to exploit purported policy differences. The Swedish socialists then did the *lagom* thing and hijacked the conservative party programme, disowning proletarian values and demolishing the welfare state in favour of a profit and loss ethic. It worked: they are now back in power.

Sweden has its share of ephemeral political movements like the Vegetarian Cannibal Party, the Ikea DIY Party and, optimistically, the Honest Politicians' Party. There are also the Greens, who not only object to nuclear power, but advocate the dismantling of Sweden's entire industrial infrastructure and a return to subsistence farming.

One of the curses of Swedish *undfallenhet* is that nobody is prepared these days to lead the country *i nöd och lust* – through thick and thin. For instance, tired of domestic politics, Prime Minister Ingvar Carlsson declared in mid-term that the job was too much of a bother and offered it to a lady minister in his cabinet. The latter was keen enough but failed to win parliamentary confirmation after a skeleton fell out of her cupboard. Nobody else wanted the job, so eventually it landed in the lap of the finance minister.

Swedish politicians, like their foreign counterparts, are masters in the art of warping the truth. But when foreign politicians lie, their body language usually gives them away. Since Swedish officials have no body language at all, there is nothing to contradict their apparent sincerity. When it comes to deceiving the public, Swedish politicians win hands down.

The Monarchy

Jean Bernadotte, a general in Napoleon's army, was head-hunted in 1810 by the Swedish nobility to succeed the incumbent King who was childless and growing senile. He nearly flunked his job interview on a point of language. During his inaugural speech before the Parliament, the audience became hysterical over his pidgin Swedish. Though he landed the job and became a highly respected monarch, he never spoke another word of Swedish.

Bernadotte did not immediately take to his new kingdom. In a letter dated 1810 he sketched a portrait of Sweden which still sounds familiar: 'The wine is awful, the people without temperament, and even the sun radiates no warmth.' His queen Désirée, arriving after her husband, received a more favourable first impression. Disembarking from her ship on the south coast, she was delighted to find herself welcomed by hundreds of farmers standing on the quay chanting "*Vive la Reine!*" in perfectly recognisable French. In actual fact nobody on the quay knew a word of French. Because of the severe drought and meagre harvest during the previous summer, the farmers were merely demanding "*Vi vill ha regn!*" ("We want rain!").

The Bernadottes founded a dynasty of distinguished regents, some with a scholarly bent. For instance, Gustav VI Adolf was a widely respected archaeologist. His grandson, the present King Carl XVI Gustav, lectures about the ecological perils of seal-hunting, especially to the Norwegians. Calls for the abolition of the Swedish monarchy are rare – at least in Sweden.

Defending the Neutrality

Sweden's stated aim is to maintain 'non-alignment in peacetime, leading to neutrality in wartime'. It is recognised that the declaration alone, however beautifully worded, will not necessarily deter belligerent countries from attacking Sweden. Neutrality has to be defended with guns, blood and, as a last resort, fermented herring.

Any potential aggressor must be made to think twice, i.e. to trade off the strategic value of an invasion against the menace of a strong defending army, navy and air force. Sweden has therefore had to build up an impressive war machine. The most awesome weapon produced domestically is the *Gripen* (Griffin), an ultra-modern combat aircraft almost entirely controlled by software, against which pilots sometimes fight a losing battle and eject to save their lives.

Sweden and the European Union

Following a national referendum, Sweden decided to join the European Union. However the ayes nearly lost out to the nays on the issue of snuff. In Europe only the Danes and the Swedes get a real kick out of snuff. The substance was threatened with a ban, leaving 800,000 Swedish snuff-takers – 10% of the population – with a stark choice on referendum day.

It would be wrong to think, however, that Sweden is not prepared to compromise. The country has, after all, a long history of compromising both Norway and Finland. However, the give-and-take is of a singularly Swedish brand. For example, having advocated total abolition of poultry battery sheds within the E.U., Sweden settled for a compromise whereby the statutory shed size was increased, and the provision of a nest, a sand bath and a perch became mandatory.

Systems

Roads

Traffic on Swedish highways is surprisingly sedate considering the latent muscle of the Volvos and Saabs, the long distances to be covered, and the runway-like standard of the highways. In fact, certain sections of Swedish country roads double as auxiliary runways for the Air Force, and aircraft have the right of way. The remaining highway network also has a runway feel to it, with its paved shoulders being almost as wide as the driving lanes themselves.

The most curious aspect of Swedish motoring is the number of people driving on the hard shoulder rather than in the main lanes. You can be in the midst of overtaking a logging truck rumbling down the shoulder, with similar behemoths approaching from the other direction, when the truck suddenly lurches into your lane to avoid some mushroom-picker's automobile parked on the said shoulder. No longer need you worry about sending postcards to your friends and relatives. You are the postcard.

Education

On a per-capita basis Sweden spends more tax money on primary and secondary education than any other country in the world. Filling square minds with rounded knowledge is a costly business. With both parents out at work, most Swedish pre-school children sharpen their elbows at day-care centres. School begins at the age of seven, compared with five in Britain and six in many other nations. Sex education has been a compulsory subject in the school curriculum since the 1950s.

During the social equalisation campaigns of the 1960s and 70s examinations and grading were removed to avoid undue scholastic pressure. Many parents approved, but the universities despaired at the prospect of having to include reading, spelling and arithmetic in the curriculum. Belatedly, society has begun to react against the notion that all children are equal in every respect. Grades have been re-introduced, and private schools offering a return to the basic three Rs are once again doing brisk business.

Among Sweden's dozen universities, the one in Uppsala is the oldest and best known internationally. Its sprawling campus is centred around the magnificent cathedral and spreads in all directions into the city proper. The students' social life converges not on fraternities or sororities but on 'Nations' representing Sweden's different provinces. The historic buildings housing the Nations are not sign-posted but a visitor can find his way just by following his nose. The smells wafting out through the National kitchens are unmistakably regional, ranging from the putrid stench of fermented herring in the Nation of the Northern Provinces to the pungent aroma of coagulated pig's blood soup in the Skåne Nation. Faced with such culinary miracles, many would-be visitors experience sudden withdrawal symptoms.

Swedish university students are confronted by most of the same problems as other students around the world, including housing shortages, career choices and unplanned pregnancies. However, tuition is free. To cover their living expenses students receive a comfortable 'student salary' of which 30% is an outright grant regardless of the parents' income or willingness to support. The remainder is repaid after graduation through a deduction from the individual's salary – if and when he or she finds a job.

The Swedish appetite for learning does not end with secondary school or university. People flock to evening classes where they study everything from Culture to Meat Cleaving and Sound Sleeping Techniques. Immigrants even earn a modest salary by attending classes to learn Swedish.

Crime and Punishment

Crime

Comparing crime rates between countries is famously difficult due to diverging definitions of crime. The Swedes believe that the most reliable comparison parameter is the number of people in prison per 1,000 inhabitants. Given that their penal system strives to minimize imprisonment, the Swedes come out tops once again.

Driving a vehicle under the influence of any amount of alcohol is a crime in Sweden. Teachers must not strike pupils, but pupils may issue death threats to their teachers with impunity. Robbing a bank with a pistol might get you into trouble for breaking the gun laws; but robbing it of tens of millions of pounds through mismanagement is all right and earns the wrongdoer a golden handshake.

Punishment

Swedish prisons are neither penitentiaries nor correctional facilities. The nearest international equivalent is Club Méditerranée.

Professional criminals are usually let off lightly. Peter Wallenberg's kidnappers were set free altogether, and Olof Palme's assassin was never even caught. The only crime which guarantees the culprit a spell behind bars is drunken driving. Consuming even a thimbleful of alcohol before hitting the road can earn the driver a prison sentence of up to two years.

Pranksters, rogues, rascals, rapscallions, speeding offenders and other perpetrators of mischief are subject not to incarceration but to slow and systematic torture. The torture instrument is known as the *dagsböter* and grabs the offender where it hurts the most: the wallet.

On the surface, the *dagsböter* is merely a fine; but

instead of establishing a set fine for a given offence, the judicial system endeavours to inflict more pain by adapting the fine to the offender's pocket. So if a rich person is caught speeding, his *dagsböter* will be much higher than that of a pauper travelling at the same speed.

There have been some interesting twists in the history of *dagsböter*. A penniless university student once pulled the handle of a public fire alarm in order to impress his girlfriend. Instead of going into hiding, he waited cheekily for the fire engines to arrive. When the fire chief discovered the prank and summoned the police, the student just stood there and laughed, knowing that his *dagsböter* would inevitably come to zero. But, unbeknown to him, his millionaire grandparents had placed a large chunk of their fortune in trust for him in order to gain tax relief. The size of the *dagsböter* wiped the smile off the face of the student but left everyone else grinning.

Business

The Swedish Model

The Swedish Model is a social formula which grew out of Sweden's balancing act between Capitalism and Communism after World War II. The resulting welfare state owes much to the strict observance of political neutrality between East and West.

With their profound sense of *lagom*, the Swedes have discovered the virtues of moderation, compromise and teamwork. Examples abound, such as the relatively peaceful coexistence between employers and trade unions, and the ease with which management delegates responsibility to the workforce. Sociologists and psychologists abroad marvel at the way the Swedes have managed to reconcile individualism and collectivism, enabling the individual to derive maximum job satisfaction without sacrificing his regard for the common good.

Other countries eyed Sweden's social experiment with awe and envy, and for decades foreign analysts and news gatherers looked for cracks in the Swedish Model. In 1992 the world sighed with satisfaction as the bottom fell out of the Swedish real-estate market, the banks nearly went bankrupt, and the *krona* lost 30% against the dollar. Unemployment began skyrocketing towards 10% and beyond. Once a beacon and a milestone for the world's social planners, the Swedish Model had become the Swedish Muddle.

But important lessons have been learned. The Swedes are rising fast from economic hell to rebuild their particular brand of a welfare paradise. When it comes to housing standards, second homes, cars, boats, personal computers and mobile phones, Sweden is already at the top of the global heap.

Work, Work, Work

The Swedes carefully nourish their Lutheran work ethic except when they are tied up in union gatherings; or taking their statutory 5 weeks of annual vacation; or doing 7 months of military service; or enjoying 15 months of maternity leave; or being on a training course. There is nothing like a good day's work, especially when the working day only happens once or twice a year.

Women make up half of the Swedish workforce, a first in the industrialised world and second only to the Third World where women do all the work. Side by side with their male colleagues, they take time off work to help raise Swedish competitiveness at home and abroad.

The Swedes enjoy going to team-building conferences at Mediterranean seaside resorts or maybe on board a cruise ship to Finland. The outing offers much sightseeing, eating, drinking and extramarital bonding at the company's expense, organised by the employer to reward the staff for their hard work.

The Incubator Culture

Sweden sports a unique 'incubator' culture where people work primarily towards self-fulfilment in an egalitarian atmosphere.

The scene is typified by Volvo and Saab. The two Swedish automobile manufacturers pioneered the 'dock assembly' process in which line assembly workers were divided into small teams which assembled entire cars from the first bolt to the last rivet. The idea was that the workers would widen their expertise on the job, identify themselves with productivity and quality goals, and derive professional satisfaction in the process – a typically Swedish preoccupation.

After a few years of chasing wrongly routed components and finding that teams working at different speeds gradually got out of sync in the overall production flow, the workers begged for mercy and were put back on traditional assembly line work.

Volvo at one point seriously contemplated another new approach to job enrichment called 'Lean Production'. The technique was to use half of everything – workers, effort, space, investment, time, and parts. This was the closest Volvo ever came to reinventing the motorcycle.

Decision Making

Foreign businessmen attending important meetings usually rely on agendas to know what is to be discussed, and on minutes to know what was decided. They find Swedish informality in these matters unsettling. Swedish business-men are equally puzzled by foreigners calling for decisions long after full agreement seems to have been reached.

While Americans want the meeting to conclude with a contract and Italians prefer it to end over lunch, the Swedes are far ahead of them all by having already settled for *lagom*, i.e. the point in the discussion when they first identified the optimum solution. The rest of the meeting is small talk, and the contract becomes a mere formality. Unfortunately only the Swedes possess the insight needed to know when *lagom* has been attained.

Yet another consequence of *undfallenhet* is the reluc-tance of people in power to exercise it. In the name of consensus, managers prefer to leave all important deci-sion-making to committees. The same goes for politi-cians. When their denigration of dictatorship and racism in far-away countries fails to topple odious governments, Swedish politicians go on television to declare that the time is ripe for 'some tough decisions' which they happily delegate to the U.N.

Then there are the 'Citizens' Associations'. These are established by law to allow local residents to influence the management of communal concerns such as water supplies, road maintenance and recreation facilities. Once upon a time there were three friendly neighbours who lived on a hillside. They formed a committee and purchased a £1,000 snow-blower with a view to the members taking it in turns to clear their shared 50-metre driveway.

The neighbour at the bottom of the hill soon got tired of the chore since he only used the first 5 metres anyway; the neighbour at the top who had a garage big enough to house the blower kept forgetting to hand over the key when he left for milder climes. The neighbour in the middle finally stationed the blower in his garden where it seized up from weather exposure, so that when the sun-tanned neighbour returned he was unable to scale the snow-bound driveway. Bitter arguments ensued. And all the time the local authority would have done the job for a mere £30 a year.

Time Keeping

Multi-tasking is an unknown concept in Sweden. Swedes are taught from early childhood to do one thing at a time, and to finish it properly before embarking on the next activity. The only problem with this approach is that, should a friend or business associate show up late for an appointment, there is an immediate domino effect on the Swede's agenda, and the rest of his day falls apart.

The Swedish businessman tends to show up 15 minutes early for business meetings, start circling the block to kill the extra time, and get arrested for kerb crawling.

Swedish punctuality is highly undervalued abroad. In France a Swedish dinner guest arriving at the stated hour is likely to catch the host in the midst of shaving and the hostess in the bath. In Spain the host and hostess are probably still recovering from the siesta. With natural grace, the Swedish guest will accept almost any apology and will wait in the living-room for the entertainment to begin. There he will sit stiffly upright in a corner of the sofa, one hand still clutching his bouquet of flowers and the other impatiently strumming the sidetable.

As the other guests begin to trickle in, the Swedish visitor is unsure whether to kiss hands, bow or shake hands. So he walks around among the latecomers wagging his forearm like a semaphore while uttering "*Hej-hej*", which is meant to sound like a jolly "Ho-ho-ho!" but could be interpreted as "Bye-bye", leaving the other guests wondering if he is coming or going.

During the dinner he spreads the foie gras on the toast in the palm of his hand. Dismayed to find himself seated to the left of the hostess, he acknowledges her scintillating conversation with absent-minded grunts, while preparing his speech. After delivering the speech, he becomes a changed man; he quaffs the wine, dives into the dessert, and even makes conversation with the hostess. From then on he is in his element regaling the other guests with the wonders of Sweden.

Time flies and booze flows when one is having fun. While the Swedish guest may have been the first to arrive at the dinner party, he won't make the mistake of being the first to leave. As soon as he embarks on the Swedish Model, however, the eyes of the host and hostess begin to glaze over. When he extols the virtues of driving with the headlights on even in daylight, the other guests are already consulting their watches. As he moves right along to the high price of petrol and alcohol in Sweden, a few rise to kiss the hostess on both cheeks. When his monologue culminates with Pavarottian renditions of Swedish drinking songs, the last guest has left.

Then the time has come for the host to stand up, wag his forearm like a semaphore and say "*Hej-hej*". As in "Bye-bye".

Language

The Swedish language is very easy to learn and can be mastered in the 2½ hours it takes to fly from London's Heathrow to Stockholm's Arlanda airport. It consists of German words arranged according to English grammar and pronounced with a roller-coaster inflection. The language has a relatively small active vocabulary, which explains why the Swedes are so taciturn and tend to repeat themselves.

A curious trend among young Swedes is to split up compound nouns. For example, *En brunhårig sjuksköterska* (A brown-haired nurse) is now written as *En brun hårig sjuk sköterska* (A brown hairy sick carer). The parents blame the truncated text message feature in cellular phones favoured by their teenagers. Older Swedes blame the Americans.

The words *svårmod*, *lagom*, *skål*, *nöff-nöff*, etc., have already been explained. Among the two dozen others that make up the rest of the vocabulary, the following are in regular use. The first four capture Swedish living and loving habits in ascending order of commitment:

Mambo denotes one who lives at home with *mamma*.

Särbo is a person who regularly sleeps with the same partner whilst living apart.

Sambo is someone who lives and sleeps with a partner without being married.

Gift means 'married', an increasingly scarce form of partnership in Sweden. By coincidence, it also means 'poison'.

Bonusbarn (bonus children) is the politically correct term for stepchildren, since they are included for free, so to speak.

Präktig, applied to a man, means fine, splendid, magnificent. A *präktig* woman, however, is a female welterweight.

Käck is what Swedish women like their boyfriends to be: dashing, intrepid, plucky – not to be confused with husband material. A *käck* person manages to keep his *svårmod* at bay for weeks on end.

Hurtig means being brisk and keen, a quality which, when added to *präktig* and *käck*, makes for a totally wholesome person who conforms to every ideal, and makes the rest of us instantly want to behave like a slob.

The Author

Peter Berlin left his native Sweden the day after graduating from university, and has always looked back since. He maintains that you have to go abroad to view your country in perspective, for how can one size up a whale from within? Of course Sweden is not a whale but a slightly fermented herring, usually delectable but sometimes hard to swallow.

His Canadian wife, a textile artist, has given him a wider focus on Sweden. When there she roams the forests in search of mushrooms for dyeing wool and places each day's harvest on the hotel room radiator to dry overnight, slowly asphyxiating her husband in the process.

But there is life in the author yet. After 25 years in the satellite and rocket business, he took early retirement to become a full-time writer. Instead, he found himself re-employed to gather intelligence at Siberian and Kazakh space centres previously unknown to the West. He also gives seminars in Cross-Cultural Awareness during which he offers living proof that your cultural luggage stays with you for life.